The SOUND SLEUTH

More Than 80 Phonics Activities for K–2

By Kylie Dunn

Illustrated by Street Level Studio
Based on Illustrations by Katie McRobert

Good Year Books

Parsippany, New Jersey

The author thanks David Corney for his help and advice in the early stages of the production of this book.

Good Year Books
are available for most basic curriculum subjects plus many enrichment areas. For more Good Year Books, contact your local bookseller or educational dealer. For a complete catalog with information about other Good Year Books, please write:

Good Year Books
An imprint of Pearson Learning
299 Jefferson Road
Parsippany, New Jersey 07054-0480
1-800-321-3106
www.pearsonlearning.com

Cover and text art copyright © 1998 Good Year Books.
Copyright © 1996 Addison Wesley Longman Australia.
Originally published in Australia as Sound Success. This Edition of Sound Success (First Edition) is published by arrangement with Addison Wesley Longman Australia PTY., Ltd., Melbourne, Australia.

All Rights Reserved.
Printed in the United States of America.

ISBN   0-673-36390-2

3 4 5 6 7 8 9 - CRK - 05 04 03 02 01 00

Only portions of this book intended for classroom use may be reproduced without permission in writing from the publisher.

CONTENTS

INTENTION and use of this BOOK

The purpose of *The Sound Sleuth* is:

1. To provide hands-on activities that support concepts generally presented in core reading programs
2. To provide ready-made student resources, such as charts and games, to save valuable teacher time
3. To promote an enjoyment of reading in children
4. To provide activities for students to complete independently or with parent volunteers

The activities in this book enable children to practice a wide variety of skills. The activities involve children in the recognition of letters, letter combinations and words, word building, and the use of basic grammar. The Teacher Notes beginning on page vi list each skill presented.

The activities vary considerably in difficulty. Teacher discretion, according to individual children in the class, should dictate the timing and use of each activity. Different groups of children can work simultaneously on different activities. Encourage fast finishers to attempt the extension activities suggested in the Teacher Notes.

All activities and games are aimed at primary level students. Activities focusing on single sounds and consonant-vowel-consonant words provide valuable practice for all primary students. Many of the skills dealing with blends and more challenging reading skills may be presented as students advance in their reading ability. Other activities may be more appropriately used to introduce or reinforce specific skills to early readers.

Generally, it is helpful to read through the Teacher Notes prior to presenting an activity to the class. Then read through the directions on each page with students to assure understanding. Construct models prior to the introduction of an activity to allow children to see the final product and understand its use.

Sound Sleuth is a motivating supplement to a core reading program. The ready-to-use activities and games creatively support the kinds of oral and written work presented at the primary level. Please refer to the Teacher Notes beginning on page vi.

From *The Sound Sleuth*. Copyright © 1998 Good Year Books.

TEACHER Notes

CONSONANTS AND SHORT VOWELS

Single Sounds Desk Chart .... *Page 1*

Skill: Letter recognition

The letter chart can be attached to each child's desk with clear tape and used as a reference to remind children of correct letter formations and sounds.

Extensions:

Move a finger from letter to letter to spell words in weekly spelling lists.

Bed .... *Page 2*

Skill: Differentiation of b and d

After making the man in the bed, form a *b* and *d* with left and right hands, using the thumbs and forefingers to make the ellipse shape in each letter. Place together to see that the *b* forms the head of the bed and the *d* the foot of the bed. Refer to students' hands when deciding how to form a *b* or *d*.

Optional Activity:

Make and decorate large *b* and *d* posters and display them on either side of the blackboard. Draw accompanying pictures beginning with *b* or *d* on each poster (e.g., a boy with a bat and ball and a dog digging in the dirt).

Sound Match Game .... *Pages 3–4*

Skill: Single sound recognition

Match the cards on page 4 with the pictures on the sound games board on page 3 before the sand in an egg-timer runs out. Alternatively, both pages can be cut up and used to play snap (turning 2 cards over and slapping matching cards) or memory (turning all cards face down and choosing two of them to try to make a match).

Farmyard Vowels–Song Sheet .... *Page 5*

Skill: Vowel recognition

Use the short vowel sound to sing the individual letters in the "Farmyard Song." After singing it through together, divide the class into five groups, each representing one of the vowel sounds. Have each vowel group sing the verse that focuses on its vowel. Repeat by singing long vowels if desired.

Vowel Puppets .... *Page 6*

Skill: Vowel recognition

Photocopy or paste this page onto tagboard. Each child decorates and makes one vowel to be used in the vowel song on page five. Alternatively, vowels can be cut out and used for a wall display.

Hidden Vowels .... *Page 7*

Skill: Vowel recognition

Children can write a vowel on each of the fingers of their nonwriting hands with markers. They can refer to their fingers when hunting for vowels in the worksheet.

Extension:

Children can list as many words as possible that contain a particular vowel as a middle sound.

Which Vowel? (a, u) .... *Page 8*

Skill: Vowel recognition

Model how the slotted sentences are made. Read the nonsense sentences created by the respective vowels and vote on which make the most sense.

Extension:

Discuss when it makes sense to use the words *sat* and *sit*.

Which Vowel? (e, i, o) .... *Page 9*

Skill: Vowel recognition

Make sentences as on page 8.

Extension:

Early finishers can make another sentence with a missing vowel for a friend to solve.

From *The Sound Sleuth*. Copyright © 1998 Good Year Books.

From *The Sound Sleuth*. Copyright © 1998 Good Year Books.

WORD FAMILIES AND CONSONANT-VOWEL-CONSONANT WORDS

Skill: Recognizing word families
Create a model of each cutout and show students how you made each one. Have students follow the directions on the page to make their own word-family cutouts.

Extension:
Enlarge each word-family figure for a class display, or make into an overhead transparency so you can complete each word family with the whole class.

Skill: Recognizing word families
Read the instructions as a class before making the hen and the jet.

Extension:
List other words ending in **en** and **et** on the wings of the hen and jet.

Skill: Recognizing word families
Model how the pin and pig are made.

Extension:
Fast workers can collect **in** and **ig** words and write them on cards. Play a game in which children "race against the clock" to sort the jumbled **in** and **ig** words onto large **in** and **ig** houses made from small cardboard boxes.

Skill: Recognizing word families
Make models of a dog and a cot.
Optional: Add fur made from cotton balls to the dog. Use care not to cover the words.

Skill: Recognizing word families
To brighten up the sun and rug, the rays and fringe could be cut from colored paper, rather than using the cutouts on this page.

Skill: Blending c-v-c *words*
Read the speech bubbles as a class. Make as many words as possible by turning the wheels. List or draw each word.

Skill: Recognizing rhyming words
Model how to fanfold each rhyme to make a book.

Extension:
Each child could choose a word ending to make up a rhyme.

Skill: Discriminating among words with different medial sounds
Read the instructions as a class. Listen to the differences between each word, and then act out each word.

Extension:
Children suggest other words that could be made by changing the middle sounds of these words.

CONSONANT BLENDS

Skill: Recognizing and sounding out two- and three-letter blends
The chart can be photocopied onto colored paper or tagboard or copied onto a white background and colored in by the children. It could then be laminated and used to practice the blends or attached to children's desks for their reference in reading activities.

Skill: Recognizing two-letter blends
Make sure children know what the pictures at the bottom of the page represent before attempting to sort them.

Extension:
Use the magnifying glass on page 86 to go on a "Blend Hunt" through dictionaries, class word lists, and so on.

Blend Game .... *Page 20*

Skill: Recognizing two- and three-letter blends

Photocopy or paste the word wheel and arrow onto tagboard. Children can make lists of words beginning with a particular blend according to where the arrow lands.

Extension:

Time the activity with an egg timer or with a child chosen to be the time-keeper, who watches the second hand of the class clock.

Adapting the Activity: Beginning readers can use the wheel to choose a blend for a dictionary search in a picture dictionary.

DIGRAPHS

Digraphs Desk Chart .... *Page 21*

Skill: Recognizing vowel and consonant digraphs

Discuss the difference between blends and digraphs. (In a blend all sounds can be heard, whereas in a digraph two or more sounds are joined to make one sound.) The chart can be attached to children's desks or laminated for use in group phonics activities.

CONSONANT DIGRAPHS

ch .... *Page 22*

Skill: Recognizing the digraph ch

Read the instructions and make a sample book as a class. The pictures on the page may give children ideas for more drawings for their own *ch* books.

Optional Activity:

Have a *ch* day and/or a *ch* party for children to bring in items or food beginning with *ch.*

sh .... *Page 23*

Skill: Recognizing the digraph sh

Brainstorm words beginning with **sh** before finding the **sh** words on the page. Make sure children know what portholes are. Finished ships could be used in a bulletin-board display.

ch and sh .... *Page 24*

Skill: Differentiating ch and sh

Practice saying **ch** and **sh.** Sound out the words on the fish together, and then complete the activity.

Extension:

Draw giant **sh** and **ch** nets from tagboard and paste magazine pictures on them of things with names beginning with these two digraphs.

Noisy th .... *Page 25*

Skill: Pronouncing voiced th

Compare voiced **th** (this) and **v.** Read the words on the page. Children can close their eyes and listen to decide whether it contains the **v** or **th** sounds.

Tongue Twisters with Noisy th and v ..*Page 26*

Skill: Differentiating voiced th and v

Say the tongue twisters together. Write a class tongue twister for the last page by listing words that begin with unvoiced **th,** such as **thing,** and words that begin with **f.** Compare the words before combining some of them into a tongue-twister sentence.

Quiet th .... *Page 27*

Skill: Recognizing and pronouncing unvoiced th

Practice saying unvoiced **th** (thing) and compare it to **f.** Read the words together before completing the activity.

Tongue Twisters with Quiet th and f ..*Page 28*

Skill: Differentiating f and th

Say the tongue twisters together. List words beginning with **f** and unvoiced **th,** and use some in a sentence as a class to complete the last panel of the book. Advanced students can make up their own tongue twisters.

Quiet and Noisy th .... *Page 29*

Skill: Differentiating voiced and unvoiced th

Practice pronouncing voiced and unvoiced **th,** noting that the mouth stays in the same position for both. Read the words on the page and decide if they are **noisy** (voiced as in **this**) or **quiet** (unvoiced as in **thin**).

From *The Sound Sleuth.* Copyright © 1998 Good Year Books.

> *Skill: Recognizing the digraph* th
>
> Use picture dictionaries or word banks to find words beginning with **th**. The magnifying glass on page 86 could be used for motivation.

> *Skill: Recognizing the digraph* wh
>
> Make the first **wh** sentence together and read each new sentence created by changing the word ending.

> *Skill: Recognizing the digraph* wh
>
> Use picture dictionaries or class-made dictionaries to find **wh** words.

> *Extension:*
>
> Advanced students can cover the whole whale with additional **wh** words.

> *Skill: Recognizing the digraph* qu
>
> Read both speech bubbles before completing the page.

> *Extension:*
>
> Go on a word hunt to confirm whether **q** and **u** are always together.

> *Skill: Recognizing the digraph* ph
>
> Explore this digraph with more fluent readers. Discuss how the **f** sound is sometimes made with **ph**. Make a sample phone together and spell out a **ph** word by touching the letters on the buttons. Children can work in pairs as one child "dials" a word or name as the other child watches and determines which word or name they are calling.

> *Skill: Recognizing the digraph* ph
>
> Make a sample camera together so children see how the photos slide through the slot from the back to the front.

> *Extension:*
>
> Hunt for pictures of **ph** words in magazines.

LONG VOWELS AND VOWEL DIGRAPHS

> *Skill: Recognizing long and short vowel sounds*
>
> Before completing the page, act out each word. Have three children are chosen who each make a sound in a consonant-vowel-consonant word. A fourth child, chosen to be "Bossy **e**," must boss the vowel into saying its name. Blend the sounds, first to make the short vowel word, and then to make the long vowel word when "Bossy **e**" stands at the end.

> *Skill: Recognizing that* y *can copy the sound of long* i *and* e
>
> Brainstorm words using the consonant **y**. Then think of words in which **y** makes the sound of long **i** or **e**.

> *Extension:*
>
> Search to discover if there are any words that do not contain a vowel or a "Copy Cat **y**."

> *Skill: Recognizing short vowels or long vowels and Copy Cat* y
>
> This page can be photocopied or pasted onto tagboard to make the cube easier to construct and more durable. Extra adult help may be necessary. List words that use each vowel as a middle sound or "Copy Cat **y**" as an end sound. Play the game in small groups, referring to the word lists where necessary.

> *Skill: Recognizing and sounding out the digraph ee*
>
> The symbol /e/ is used on this page to represent the long **e** sound. Help children differentiate between the sound each short vowel makes (a, e, i, o, u) and name of the vowel *(a, e, i, o, u)*.

Skill: *Recognizing and sounding out the digraph* ea

Before completing this page, introduce children to the rule "When two vowels go walking, the first one does the talking and it usually says its name."

Extension:

Search for words in dictionaries containing **ea** and find exceptions to the rule that **ea** usually makes a long e sound (e.g., **bread**).

Skill: *Recognizing and sounding the digraph* oo

Extension:

Have children suggest words containing **oo** and consider whether each digraph is making the sound it makes in **moon** or the sound it makes in **book.** In groups, compile word lists for both **oo** sounds.

Skill: *Recognizing and sounding out the digraph* oo

Cut out the page for the **oo** book and staple it together at the top or the sides.

Skill: *Recognizing and sounding the digraph* ar

Hang the stars with the moons made from page 41 in a mobile to remind children of the **oo** and **ar** digraphs.

Extension:

Collect **ar** words and write them on a large cardboard "**ar** car" and display on a bulletin board.

SILENT LETTERS

Skill: *Recognizing silent letters*

Cut and paste hands over the mouths on the silent letters. Read the words with and without pronouncing the silent letters. Compare by listening for how different each word sounds when the silent letters are pronounced.

Skill: *Recognizing silent letters*

Sort words containing silent **w, b,** or **k** into their correct pockets.

Extension:

Find words in books or on class posters and charts that contain silent letters and add them to the silent-letter pockets.

HARD AND SOFT *C* AND *G*

Skill: *Sounding out words with hard and soft* g

Read the words together as a class, listening for soft **g** sounds (as in **giraffe**) and hard **g** sounds (as in **glove**), and sort the words accordingly.

Skill: *Sounding out words with hard and soft* c

Have children add more words to each scene.

Extension:

Find other words or cut out pictures of words containing **c.** Sort and paste onto giant murals of city and country life.

WORD BUILDING

Skill: *Recognizing root words and endings*

Model folding and cutting the slotted sentences.

Skill: *Recognizing root words and endings*

Trace the words made from the first tree. Follow this example to build words using the root words and endings on the other trees.

From *The Sound Sleuth.* Copyright © 1998 Good Year Books.

From *The Sound Sleuth.* Copyright © 1998 Good Year Books.

s, es **Book** .... *Page 50*
Skill: Recognizing root words and endings
Cut out the root words and staple them in front of the *s* and *es.* Flip the pages and read the words.

Extension:
Find other root words ending with *ch, sh, ss, zz,* and *x.*

Discuss:
Does it sound better to add *s* or *es* to these words? Is there a rule or pattern for adding *s* or *es?* (When a word ends in *h, s,* or *x,* add *es.*)

ing, ed **Word Wheel** .... *Page 51*
Skill: Recognizing root words and endings
Follow the directions to make the word wheel. List words made by adding *ed* or *ing* to the root words.

Adding *ing* .... *Page 52*
Skill: Taking off e *to add* ing
Read the speech bubbles in the illustration and slide the word-ending strip down to see how *e* disappears and is replaced by *ing.* Demonstrate first if necessary.

Extension:
Discuss how final *e* also disappears when *ed, er,* and *est* are added to a root word.

ed, ing **Word Wheel** .... *Page 53*
Skill: Doubling final consonant before adding ing *and* ed *to some root words*
This activity is more suitable for more advanced primary students.

Discuss:
Observe that when a consonant is standing by itself after a short vowel at the end of a root word (e.g., *big*), it invites its twin to stand beside it before an *er, est, ing,* or *ed* ending is added.

er, est **Trees** .... *Page 54*
Skill: Recognizing root words and endings
Cross *er* or *est* off the words on the page.

er, est **Cards** .... *Page 55*
Skill: Recognizing root words and endings
Photocopy the page onto tagboard. Cut out and add the *er* and *est* cards to each of the root words.

Extension:
List the new words made by putting the cards together.

er, est **Comparisons** .... *Pages 56–57*
Skill: Recognizing root words and endings
Follow the examples in the illustration to make posters. Display them on a bulletin board.

Extension:
Observe what happens to the root words *big* and *thin* before the endings are added.

Discuss:
Double the final consonant before adding an ending to a one-syllable word.

PREFIXES

Prefix *a* .... *Page 58*
Skill: Recognizing prefixes and root words
This activity would be more suitable for advanced primary students. Discuss how a prefix can be added to the beginning of a word to change the word.

Prefix *re* .... *Page 59*
Skill: Recognizing prefixes and root words
Read the speech bubbles in the illustration to help children understand the effect of the prefix *re* on a root word. Try dramatizing the words without and with the prefix; for example, *tie* and then *retie,* or *write* then *rewrite.*

COMPOUND WORDS

Compound Words Flip Book .... *Page 60*
Skill: Recognizing compound words
List words made by flipping the pages of the compound-word book.

Extension:
Race against the clock to find and list 16 words using the flip book.

Compound Words Card Game .... *Page 61*
Skill: Recognizing compound words
Photocopy or paste the page onto tagboard before cutting. "Beat the clock" to match words or match the cards in a game of memory or snap with a partner.

CONTRACTIONS

Contractions .... *Pages 62–63*
Skill: Recognizing and making contractions
Follow the directions to make the letters from the two words disappear to change them into one word. A similar activity can be done on the chalkboard by erasing letters while the children say a magic word. A "magic apostrophe" is left behind where the letters were.

Contractions Card Match .... *Page 64*
Skill: Recognizing contractions
Photocopy or paste the page onto tagboard before cutting. Race against the clock or against a partner to match words and their contractions.

WORD SKILLS AND GRAMMAR

Syllable Drums.................................... *Page 65*
Skill: Recognizing and counting syllables
Draw dots on the drums representing beats made by the drumsticks. Alternatively, numerals could be written on each drum according to the number of syllables in each word.

Extension:
Hunt for and list words with a given number of syllables.

Syllable Claps .... *Page 66*
Skill: Recognizing and counting syllables
Clap out the names of children in the class, counting the syllables in each. Children can then choose five of the names to write on the hands.

Opposite Match........................... *Pages 67–68*
Skill: Recognizing and matching antonyms
Photocopy or paste the pages onto tagboard before cutting out. Match the cards in a game of snap or memory.

Synonym Book.................................... *Page 69*
Skill: Recognizing synonyms
Define **synonyms** as words with the **same meaning**. Read the directions as a class and construct a sample book. Extra adult help may be needed when children are cutting and folding their own books. Illustrate the pages after the book has been folded.

Homonym Poster .... *Page 70*
Skill: Recognizing homonyms
Define **homonyms** as words that **sound the same**. Follow the example in the illustration to make posters to display.

Extension:
Brainstorm other words that have different meanings but sound the same.

Two or To .... *Page 71*
Skill: Differentiating two *and* to
Color and complete the worksheet.

Extension:
In groups, write other sentences containing **two** or **to**. Publish the sentences on a chart, which can be used later for reference in writing stories.

Too (As Well) .... *Page 72*
Skill: Differentiating to *and* too
Give examples of the use of the word **to** ("I am going to a party."). Then discuss one meaning of the word **too** ("as well," e.g., "May I come too?"). Discuss the use of the word **too** in the illustration. Choose whether **to** or **too** makes more sense in each sentence.

To or Too (More than Enough) .... *Page 73*
Skill: Differentiating to *and* too
Read the speech bubbles and discuss another meaning of the word **too** ("more than enough," e.g., "too cold" or "too hard"). Cut and paste **to** or **too** into the correct boxes.

From *The Sound Sleuth.* Copyright © 1998 Good Year Books.

From *The Sound Sleuth*. Copyright © 1998 Good Year Books.

Skill: Recognizing adjectives
Define adjectives as words that describe something or someone (or simply use the term "describing words"). Make the slotted sentence with adjectives for Watson.

Optional Activity:
Describe things around the room or children in the class and list the words suggested.

Skill: Recognizing the terms true *or* false
Define *true* and *false* as *right* and *wrong* before completing the page.

Extension:
Write lists of things that are true and false on the back of the sheet.

PUNCTUATION AND SENTENCE STRUCTURE

Skill: Understanding the use of periods
Read sentences from books together. Have children raise their hands when a pause is heard or make small stop signs to hold up. Discuss how periods replace the stop signs.

Skill: Understanding the use of question marks
Read through the riddles together and solve using the picture clues if necessary. The children could circle the question and question mark in each riddle one color and the answer in another color.

Extension:
Have children make their own books of riddles to read to the class. Make sure they use question marks in each one.

Skill: Understanding the use of question marks
Read the questions together. Point out the question marks before completing the page.

Extension:
Write questions (with question marks) for a partner to answer.

Skill: Understanding the use of speech marks
Act out sentences with one child playing the part of the reader and another the part of the speaker. The masks on pages 84 and 85 could be used.

Extension:
Record a conversation children make up on the board using quotation marks.

Skill: Understanding the use of quotation marks
Write a sentence containing speech on a sentence strip and cut out each word. (Write a period after the final word and a comma after the speech, but leave out speech marks). Hand out the word cards randomly to individual children who must then order themselves so the sentence makes sense. Have two children holding the opening and closing speech mark signs on this page join the sentence at either side of the spoken section.

Extension:
Raise and lower speech mark signs where appropriate as a reader reads aloud a story.

Skill: Understanding the use of exclamation marks
Read the speech bubbles together and then follow the directions to complete the page.

Extension:
Make a list of things you might call out using exclamation marks, such as *Help!, Ouch!, Hooray!,* or *Wow!*

From *The Sound Sleuth*. Copyright © 1998 Good Year Books.

Word Families (*en*, *et*)

Name _____   **Date** _____

What to Do

1. Add **en** and **et** to make words.
2. Cut out the pieces.
3. Slide the wings through the slots in the hen and the jet.

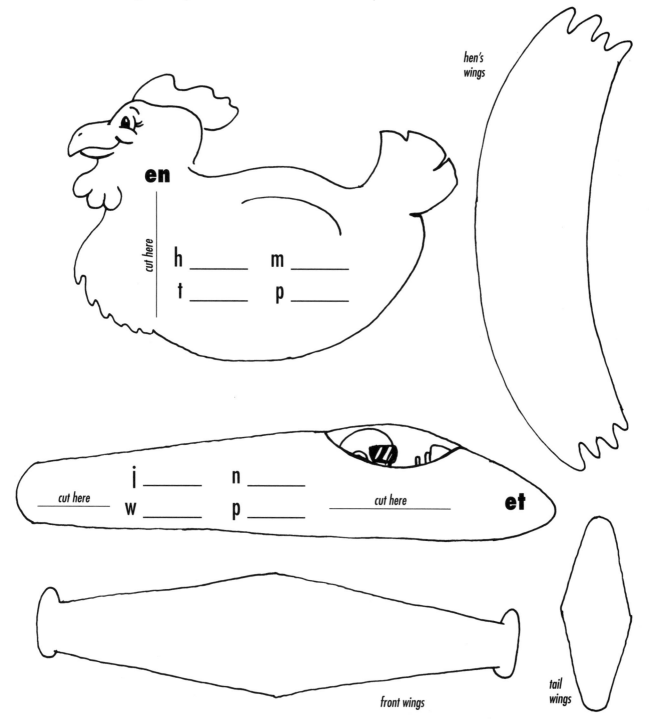

hen's wings

en

cut here

h _____   m _____
t _____   p _____

cut here   j _____   n _____   cut here   **et**
w _____   p _____

front wings

tail wings

From *The Sound Sleuth*. Copyright © 1998 Good Year Books.

Word Families (*in, ig*)

Name _____   **Date** _____

What to Do

1. Add **in** and **ig** to make words.
2. Cut out the pin and the pig.

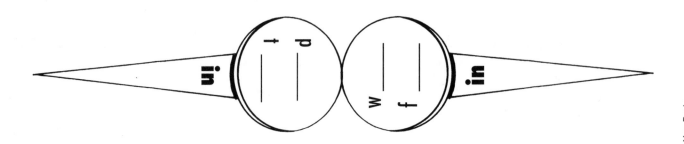

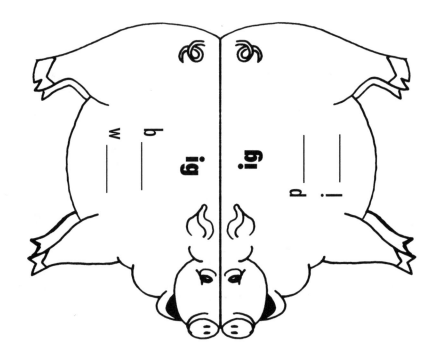

From *The Sound Sleuth.* Copyright © 1998 Good Year Books.

Word Families (*og, ot*)

Name _____   **Date** _____

What to Do

1. Add **og** and **ot** to make words.
2. Cut out the dog and the cot.

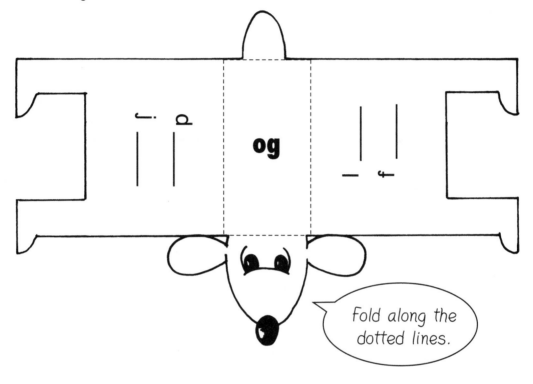

Fold along the dotted lines.

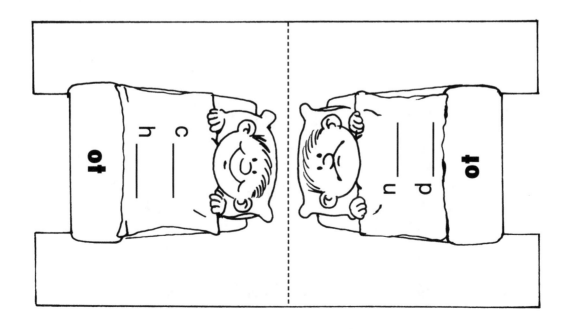

From *The Sound Sleuth*. Copyright © 1998 Good Year Books.

Word Families (*un, ug*)

Name _____   **Date** _____

What to Do

1. Add **un** and **ug** to make words.
2. Cut out the pieces.
3. Paste the rays onto the sun and the fringe onto the rug.

Sun's Rays

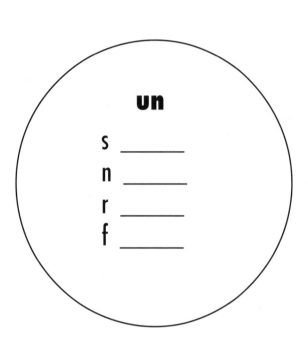

un

s _____
n _____
r _____
f _____

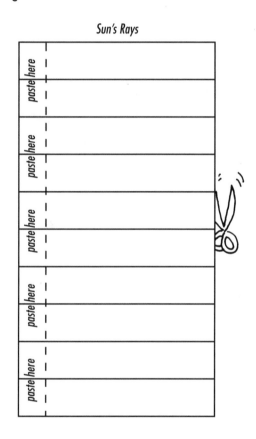

paste here

paste here

paste here

paste here

paste here

Rug's Fringe

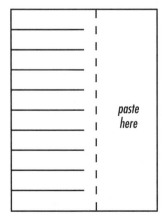

paste here

ug

r _____   h _____
b _____   m _____

paste here

From *The Sound Sleuth.* Copyright © 1998 Good Year Books.

Make a Word Wheel

Name _____   **Date** _____

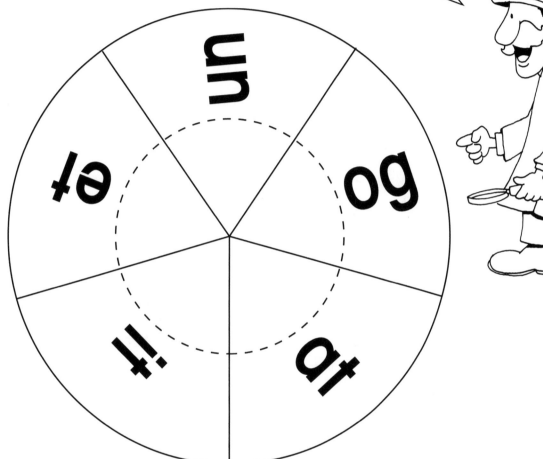

Cut out the circles and attach them at the centers with a brad.

See how many words you can make by turning the wheels.

From *The Sound Sleuth*. Copyright © 1998 Good Year Books.

Rhyming Words

Name _____   **Date** _____

Add the word endings. Then cut along the dark lines and
fold along the dotted lines to make books of rhymes.

an	D___ and J___ r___ to the v___.	
et	Don't l___ the p___ g___ w___!	
ig	The b___ p___ in the w___ did a j__.	
og	Did you see the d___ try to j___ on the l___?	
un	It's lots of f___ to r___ in the s___.	

From *The Sound Sleuth*. Copyright © 1998 Good Year Books.

Word Discrimination

Name _____   **Date** _____

Color the word that goes with each picture.

lost list	hot hit

pig peg	map mop

bin bun	cap cup

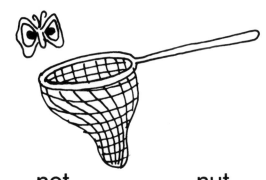 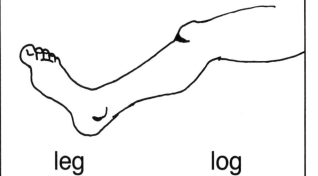

net nut	leg log

From *The Sound Sleuth.* Copyright © 1998 Good Year Books.

Consonant Blends Desk Chart

Name _____

Date _____

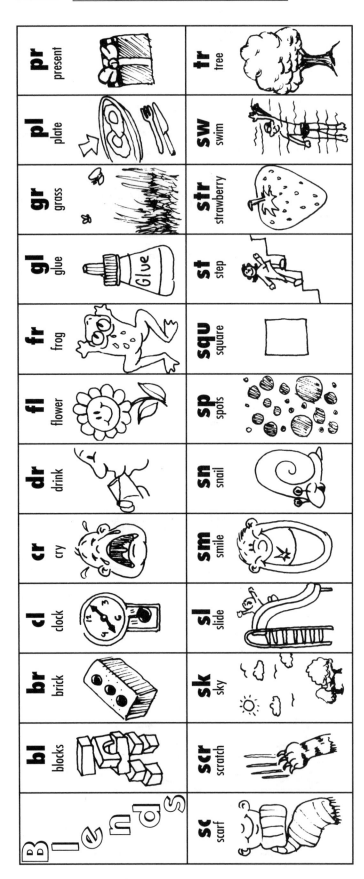

pr present		**tr** tree	
pl plate		**sw** swim	
gr grass		**str** strawberry	
gl glue		**st** step	
fr frog		**squ** square	
fl flower		**sp** spots	
dr drink		**sn** snail	
cr cry		**sm** smile	
cl clock		**sl** slide	
br brick		**sk** sky	
bl blocks		**scr** scratch	
Blends		**sc** scarf	

Use this desk chart to help you remember the two- and three-letter blends.

From *The Sound Sleuth.* Copyright © 1998 Good Year Books.

Blend Hunt

Name _____   **Date** _____

Find pictures of words beginning with **_br_**, **_cr_**, and **_dr_** and paste them in the right boxes.

br	cr	dr

From *The Sound Sleuth*. Copyright © 1998 Good Year Books.

Blend Game

Name _____ **Date** _____

Spin the arrow. Look at the blend you land on. In one minute write or draw as many words as you can that begin with the blend.

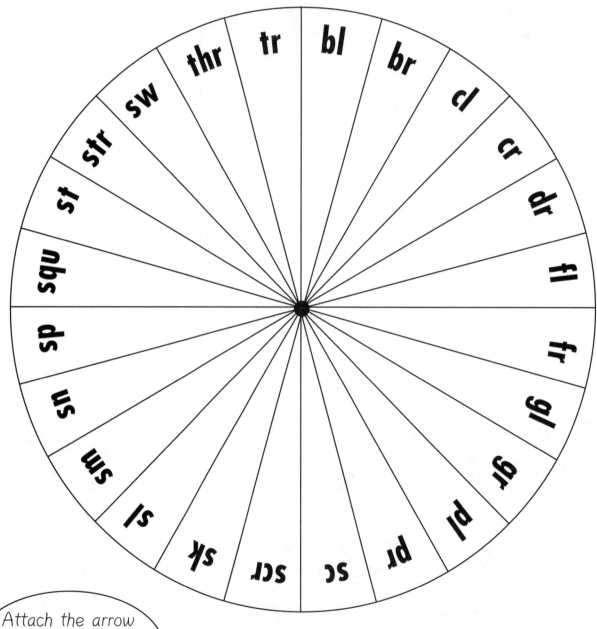

Attach the arrow to the center of the circle with a brad.

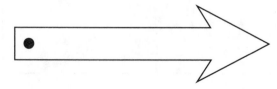

From *The Sound Sleuth*. Copyright © 1998 Good Year Books.

Digraphs Desk Chart

Name _____   **Date** _____

ew new	**ow** cow	**wh** whistle
er tiger	**ou** round	**th** thin
ei weigh	**oo** book	**sh** ship
ee see	**oo** boot	**qu** queen
ea sea	**oy** boy	**ph** photo
ay pay	**oi** point	**kn** knife
aw paw	**oe** toe	**gn** gnome
ar bark	**oa** boat	**ck** duck
au caught	**ir** first	**ch** chin
ai paint	**ie** pie	**ur** nurse
Digraphs	**ey** key	**or** fork

When two letters sit together and make one sound they are called a digraph. Use this desk chart to help you remember the digraphs.

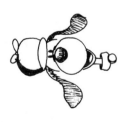

From *The Sound Sleuth.* Copyright © 1998 Good Year Books.

ch

Name _____ **Date** _____

Draw pictures and staple the pages together to make a *ch* book.

ch

ase

in

at

eese

ick

op

Look at the chick chasing the cheese!

He has a long chin!

From *The Sound Sleuth*. Copyright © 1998 Good Year Books.

sh

Name _____   **Date** _____

What to Do

1. Paste the **sh** words on the ship.
2. Find 3 extra **sh** words in a dictionary.
3. Paste the portholes and waves on the ship.

They always say that when they're together.

Why are they saying "sh"?

ship	sat	sun	shell	she	school
so	sad	shut	six	sip	sheep	dish

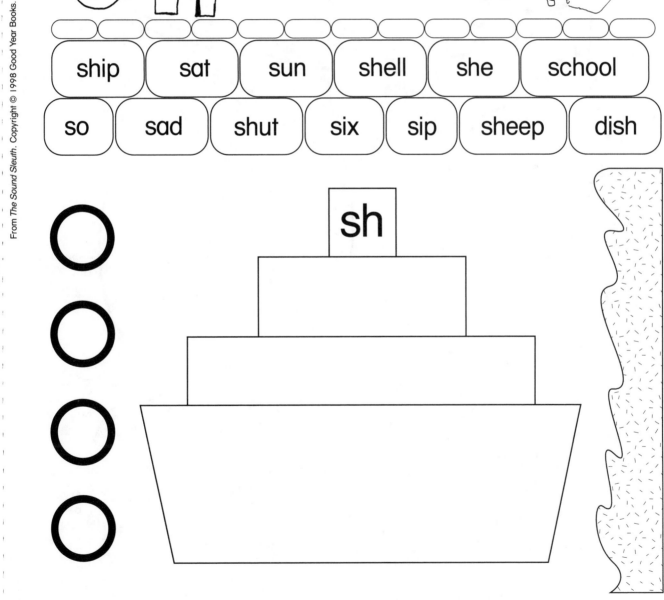

sh

From *The Sound Sleuth.* Copyright © 1998 Good Year Books.

ch and sh

Name _____   **Date** _____

We're fishing for **ch** and **sh** words.

Cut out the fish and paste them on the right net.

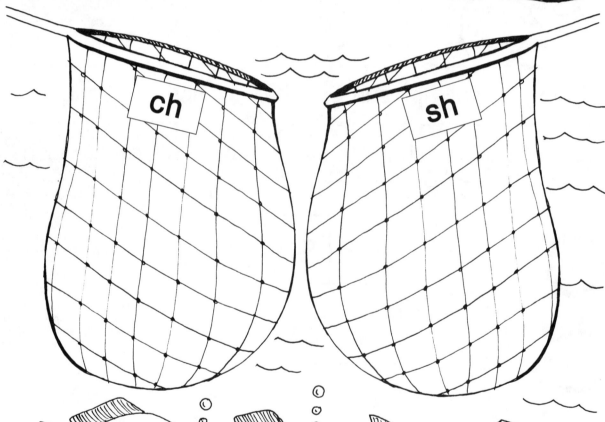

ch   **sh**

cheese   wish   ship   catch

shark   fish   chop   chin

From *The Sound Sleuth*. Copyright © 1998 Good Year Books.

Noisy *th*

Name _____   **Date** _____

Circle words with the noisy *th* sound and read them to a friend.

this	mother	van	never
the	father	very	that
video	they	those	love

From *The Sound Sleuth*. Copyright © 1998 Good Year Books.

Tongue Twisters with Noisy *th* and *v*

Name _____   **Date** _____

Draw pictures for the tongue twisters and staple the pages together.

th and **V**

Tongue Twisters

Name:

_____

Have you ever found a leather feather?

I have another clever brother.

They never like the windy weather.

They'd rather move in the other van.

My Own Tongue Twister

From *The Sound Sleuth*. Copyright © 1998 Good Year Books.

Quiet *th*

Name _____   **Date** _____

They're a lot quieter than the other **t** and **h**.

Write the words with the quiet **th** sound in the bathtub.

fall	thing	moth	fox	bath
thin	gift	with	frog	teeth

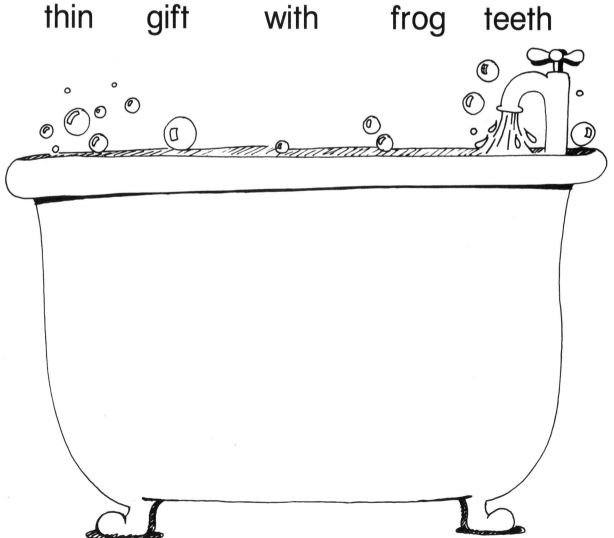

From *The Sound Sleuth*. Copyright © 1998 Good Year Books.

Tongue Twisters with Quiet *th* and *f*

Name _____ **Date** _____

Draw pictures for the tongue twisters and staple the pages together.

_____

th and f

Tongue Twisters

Name:

_____

_____

Three flies flew fast.

_____

I think that fish is funny.

_____

There's a frog in my throat.

_____

Fred found a thick thread.

_____

My Own Tongue Twister

From *The Sound Sleuth*. Copyright © 1998 Good Year Books.

Quiet and Noisy *th*

Name _____   **Date** _____

Put the quiet and noisy **th** words into the right houses.

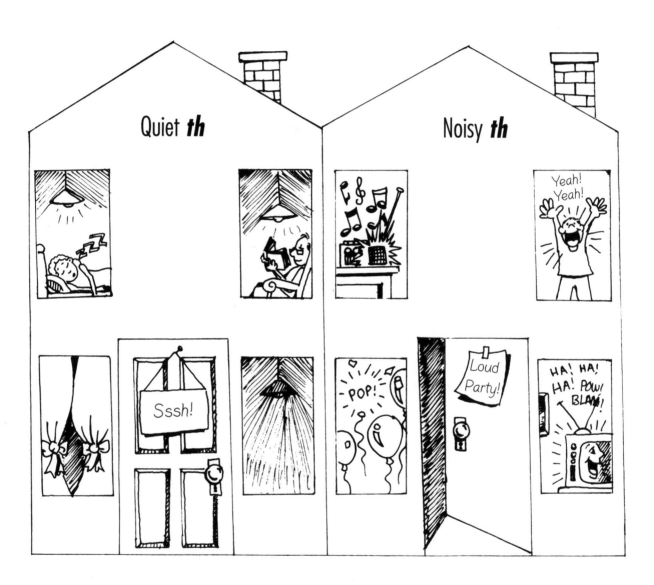

Quiet *th*

Noisy *th*

thing	this	that	threw
moth	with	they	both
thin	thumb	then	other

From *The Sound Sleuth*. Copyright © 1998 Good Year Books.

th

Name _____ **Date** _____

Find *th* words in a dictionary and write them in the three-headed thing.

Attach string here

Three-Headed Thing

From *The Sound Sleuth*. Copyright © 1998 Good Year Books.

wh Sentences

Name _____   **Date** _____

Great! I like sentence games!

So do I! Just slide the word ending strip through the slots.

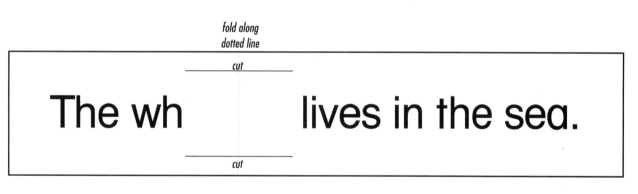

ite   en   ale   y   at   ich

fold along dotted line
cut

The wh   lives in the sea.

cut

fold along dotted line
cut

Wh   is your name?

cut

fold along dotted line
cut

Her ball is black and wh   .

cut

From *The Sound Sleuth*. Copyright © 1998 Good Year Books.

wh Whale

Name _____ **Date** _____

Find **wh** words in the dictionary and write them in the drops coming from the whale's blowhole.

From *The Sound Sleuth*. Copyright © 1998 Good Year Books.

qu

Name _____   **Date** _____

Color the **qu** in these words and draw pictures for each word.

quiet
quick
queen
quack
question
quiz

From *The Sound Sleuth*. Copyright © 1998 Good Year Books.

ph Phones

Name _____   **Date** _____

When **p** and **h** are together they make an **f** sound.

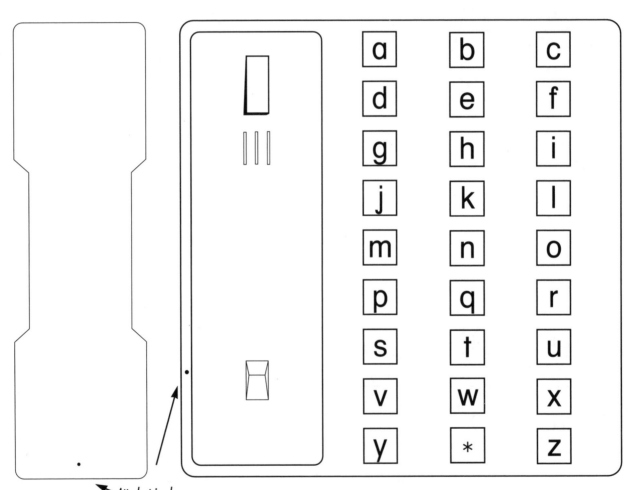

a	b	c
d	e	f
g	h	i
j	k	l
m	n	o
p	q	r
s	t	u
v	w	x
y	*	z

← *Attach string here*

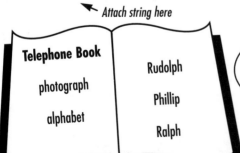

Telephone Book

photograph

alphabet

Rudolph

Phillip

Ralph

Cut out the phone. Then press the buttons to spell the words in the telephone book.

From *The Sound Sleuth.* Copyright © 1998 Good Year Books.

ph Photos

Name _____   **Date** _____

From *The Sound Sleuth*. Copyright © 1998 Good Year Books.

We make the same sound.

That's right!

Make photos by drawing pictures of the **p h** words.
Slide the photo strip through the slot in the camera.

Example:

Camera

slot

ph photos
telephone
elephant
graph

Bossy e

Name _____   **Date** _____

Draw pictures for these *Bossy e* words.

I make the vowels say their names.

*Oh no! It's Bossy **e**. My name is **a**.*

cake	face
bike	kite
nose	bone

From *The Sound Sleuth*. Copyright © 1998 Good Year Books.

Copy Cat y

Name _____   **Date** _____

Find the words that use copy cat y and paste them on your giant **y**.

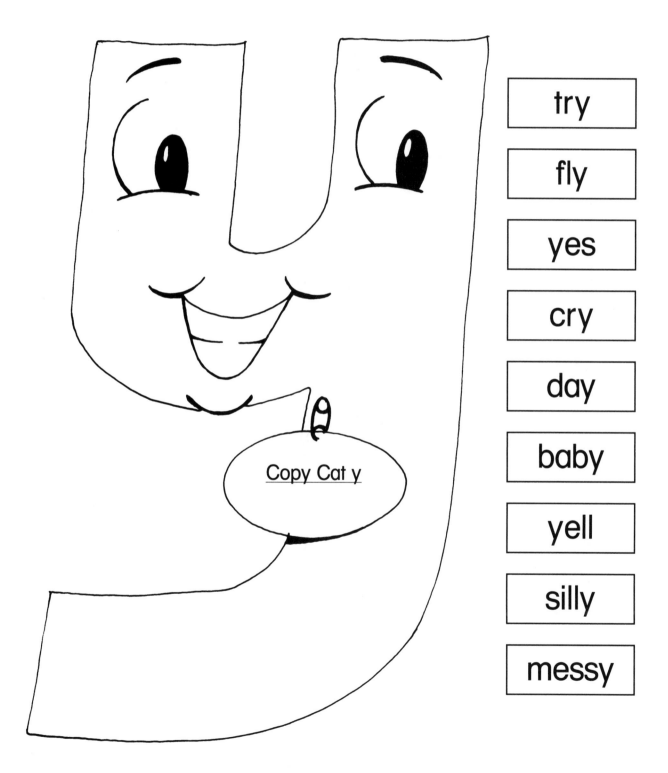

Copy Cat y

try

fly

yes

cry

day

baby

yell

silly

messy

From *The Sound Sleuth*. Copyright © 1998 Good Year Books.

Vowel Cube

Name _____   **Date** _____

fold flaps under

cut →

a

e   o   i

fold flaps under   fold flaps under

u

Copy Cat

y

Let's make a vowel cube.

Roll the cube and say a word that uses the vowel on top.

PASTE

From *The Sound Sleuth*. Copyright © 1998 Good Year Books.

ee

Name _____   **Date** _____

fet

When **e** and **e** are together they say the name of **e**.

Why are they saying their name?

I wasn't being bossy this time.

Write the **ee** words in the beetle's feet.

see	egg	tree	pen	seen
met	meet	feet	wet	deep

From *The Sound Sleuth.* Copyright © 1998 Good Year Books.

ea

Name _____ **Date** _____

From *The Sound Sleuth*. Copyright © 1998 Good Year Books.

oo Moon

Name _____   **Date** _____

Write *oo* in these words.

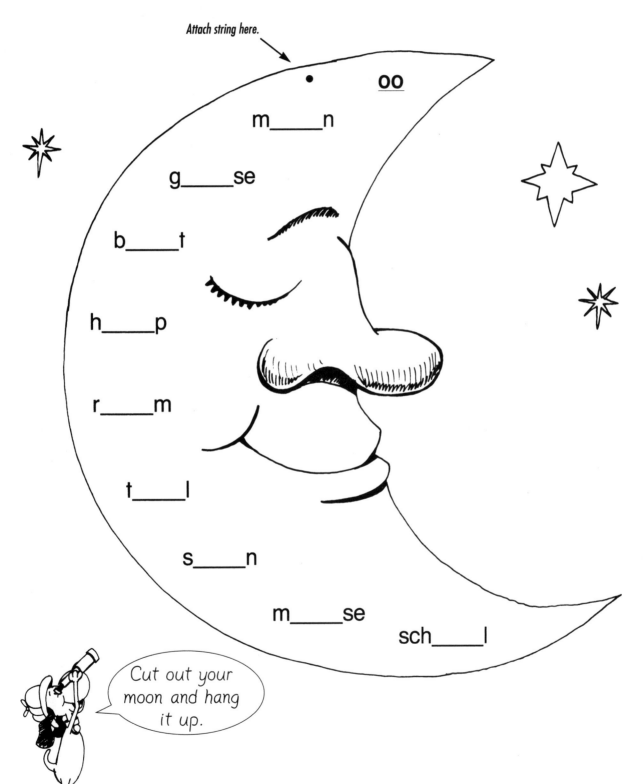

Attach string here.

oo

m____n

g____se

b____t

h____p

r____m

t___l

s____n

m____se

sch____l

Cut out your moon and hang it up.

From *The Sound Sleuth.* Copyright © 1998 Good Year Books.

oo Book

Name _____ **Date** _____

oo can make a sound like the oo in book. Draw pictures for the oo words in this book.

look		**wood**	
book		**cook**	
foot	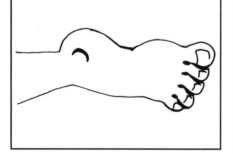	**hook**	
Name:	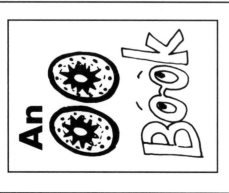	**good**	

From *The Sound Sleuth.* Copyright © 1998 Good Year Books.

ar

Name _____   **Date** _____

Write **ar** in these words.

c____

st____

f____m

b____

____m

f____

____t

c____t

p____t

d____k

From *The Sound Sleuth.* Copyright © 1998 Good Year Books.

Silent Letter Hunt

Name _____ **Date** _____

Oh, no! The silent letters are sounding off! Quick! Cover them with a hand so they can't make a sound.

Make the letters silent, and then say the words.

From *The Sound Sleuth*. Copyright © 1998 Good Year Books.

Silent Letter Pockets

Name _____   **Date** _____

Staple pockets for silent letters. Then cut out the words and place each one in its correct pocket.

Silent W

Silent B

Silent K

From *The Sound Sleuth*. Copyright © 1998 Good Year Books.

knot	crumb	knock	wrist
know	wriggle	thumb	wrong
comb	knife	who	lamb
knit	write	climb	wreck

Hard and Soft *g*

Name _____ **Date** _____

Write the words with hard **g** in the <u>hard **g** glove</u> and the words with the soft **g** in the <u>soft **g** giraffe</u>.

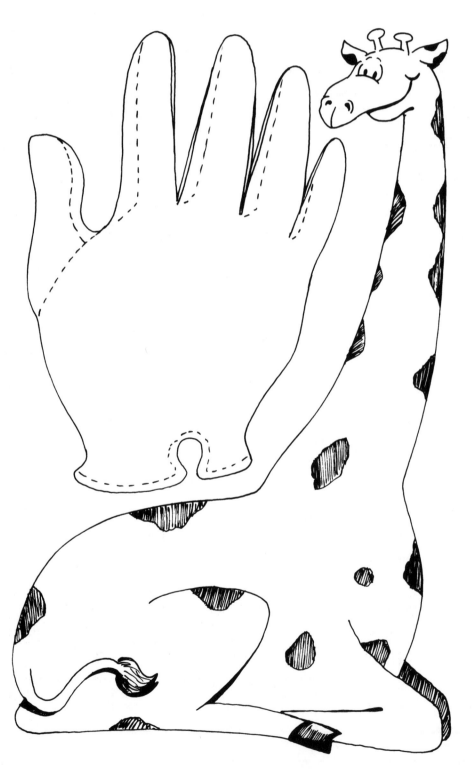

| girl |
| age |
| guess |
| gate |
| gem |
| gentle |
| gift |
| oranges |
| big |
| change |
| giant |
| go |

From *The Sound Sleuth.* Copyright © 1998 Good Year Books.

Hard and Soft c

Name _____ **Date** _____

Cut out these words and paste them in the <u>hard **c**</u> country or the <u>soft **c**</u> city.

city	race	cat
cake	coat	cent
rice	can	country
ice	nice	car

Hard **c** Country

Soft **c** City

From *The Sound Sleuth.* Copyright © 1998 Good Year Books.

s, ed, ing Slotted Sentences

Name _____   **Date** _____

Slide the word-ending strip through the slots in the sentences.

s   ed   ing

fold along dotted line

cut

She is play   with a ball.

cut

fold along dotted line

cut

He walk   down the path.

cut

fold along dotted line

cut

She ride   to school.

cut

Decide which ending makes sense in each sentence.

From *The Sound Sleuth*. Copyright © 1998 Good Year Books.

ed, ing, s Trees

Name _____ **Date** _____

What words can you make by adding endings to the root words?

walk

| walked |
| walking |
| walks |

jump

play

help

From *The Sound Sleuth*. Copyright © 1998 Good Year Books.

s, es Book

Name _____ **Date** _____

Staple the pages to make an **s** book and an **es** book.

staple here

s

| skip | hop | pat |

| cut | run | jog |

es

| catch | wish | fox |

| fizz | guess | box |

From *The Sound Sleuth*. Copyright © 1998 Good Year Books.

ing, ed Word Wheel

Name _____   **Date** _____

Cut out circles and attach them at the centers with a split pin.

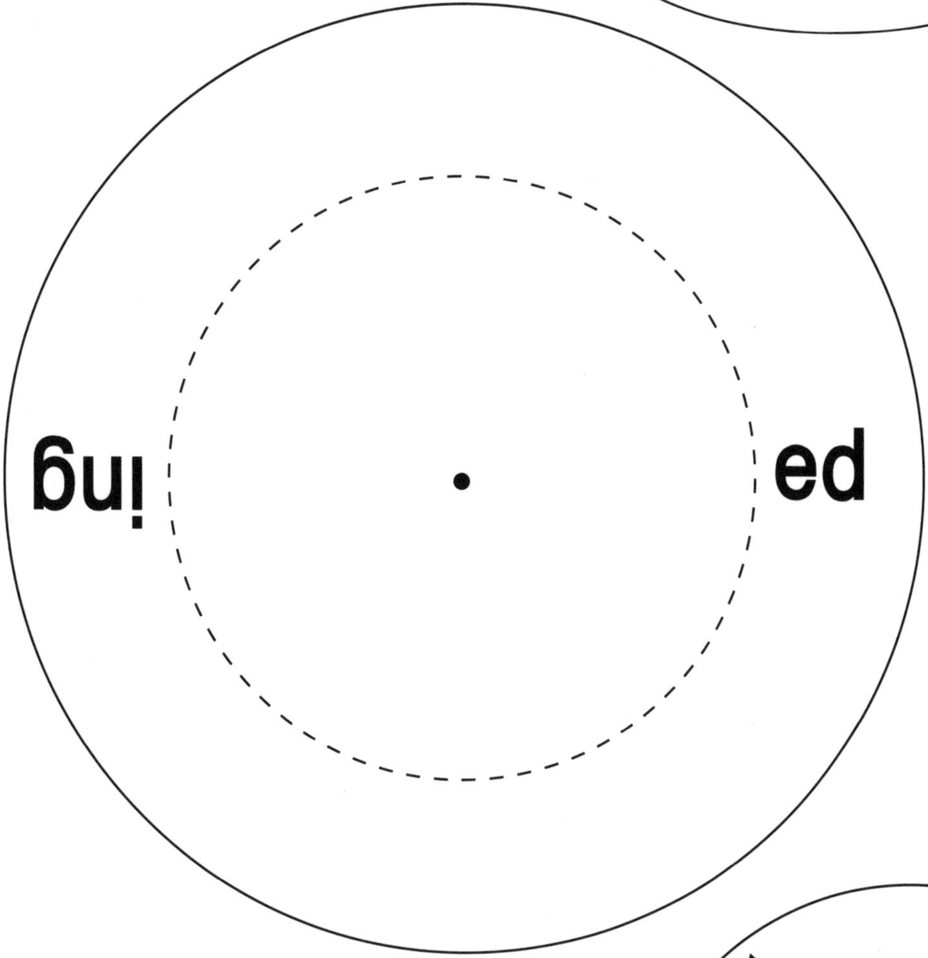

ing

ed

Turn the wheel to add **ing** and **ed** to the root words.

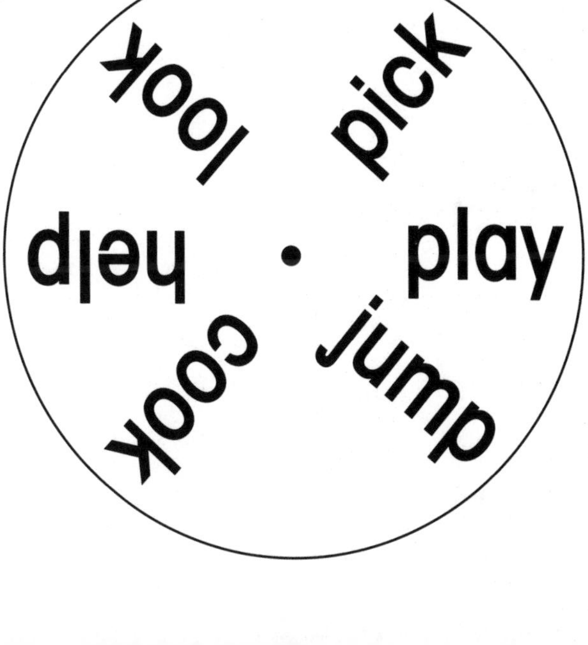

look   pick
help   play
cook   jump

From *The Sound Sleuth*. Copyright © 1998 Good Year Books.

Adding *ing*

Name _____   **Date** _____

Where is he going?

e always disappears when **ing** comes in.

Slide the strip through the slots in these words to change *e* into **ing**.

e ing
e ing
e ing
e ing
e ing

mak _____

hop _____

clos _____

shin _____

From *The Sound Sleuth*. Copyright © 1998 Good Year Books.

ed, ing Word Wheel

Name _____   **Date** _____

Sometimes we must double the last consonant before adding **ed** or **ing**.

pat

skip · hop

pot

t

d · p

d

Attach the wheels in the center and turn them to make words ending in **ed** and **ing**.

ed ing

ing
ed · ed
ing

ing ed

From *The Sound Sleuth*. Copyright © 1998 Good Year Books.

er, est Tree

Name _____   **Date** _____

Circle the root words in these words. Write them on the roots of the root word tree.

shorter hardest smallest higher lower

slowest quieter thicker quickest tallest

From *The Sound Sleuth*. Copyright © 1998 Good Year Books.

er, est Cards

Name _____   **Date** _____

Match the root-word cards with the **er** and **est** cards to make new words.

fast	small	slow
quiet	loud	tall
short	soft	hard

er	est	er	est	er	est
er	est	er	est	er	est
er	est	er	est	er	est

From *The Sound Sleuth*. Copyright © 1998 Good Year Books.

er, est Comparisons

Name _____ **Date** _____

Make a thin, thinner, and thinnest poster.

thin

thinner

thinnest

From *The Sound Sleuth*. Copyright © 1998 Good Year Books.

er, est Comparisons

Name _____   **Date** _____

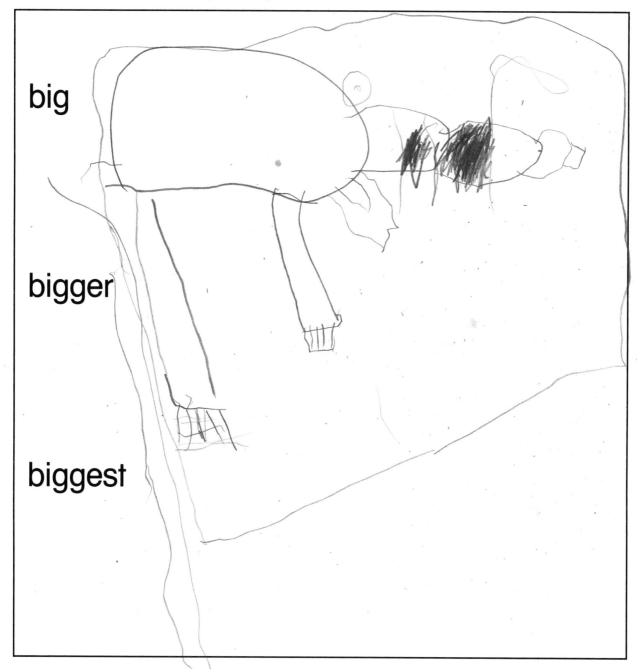

I'm big.

I'm bigger.

I'm the biggest!

Make a your own big, bigger, and biggest poster.

big

bigger

biggest

From *The Sound Sleuth*. Copyright © 1998 Good Year Books.

Prefix a

Name _____ **Date** _____

Staple these words next to the **a**. Flip the pages and read the new words.

| a | _____ |

long	round
cross	part
live	way
head	wake

From *The Sound Sleuth*. Copyright © 1998 Good Year Books.

Prefix *re*

Name _____ **Date** _____

Would you <u>replay</u> that record, Watson?

What does <u>replay</u> mean?

He wants you to <u>play it again</u>.

Underline **_re_** in these words and circle the root word.

rewind	replay	rethink
retie	reappear	redo
remake	rewrite	restart

From *The Sound Sleuth*. Copyright © 1998 Good Year Books.

Compound Words Flip Book

Name _____ **Date** _____

Staple the pages on the blackboard and flip them to make different compound words.

Left **chalkboard** *Right*

left pages	right pages
no	one
any	where
some	body
every	thing

From *The Sound Sleuth*. Copyright © 1998 Good Year Books.

Compound Words Card Game

Name _____   **Date** _____

Match the word cards to make compound words.

bath	Compound Word Game	side
flag	room	rain
coat	ball	cake
foot	tub	pan
corn	pole	pop
sun	sun	any
bed	cake	rise
cup	out	birth
shine	day	one

From *The Sound Sleuth.* Copyright © 1998 Good Year Books.

Contractions

Name _____   **Date** _____

Let's make some letters disappear!

Paste an apostrophe tab over the **i**. Say **abracadabra** and fold the tab down to make the **i** disappear.

Paste tab here	
he is	**'**
she is	**'**
it is	**'**
where is	**'**
who is	**'**

From *The Sound Sleuth*. Copyright © 1998 Good Year Books.

Contractions

Name _____   **Date** _____

Make two words into one word.
Cut out the [rebus: `,`] and paste over
the underlined letters.

Paste here # I am `,`	*Paste here* # he has `,`
Paste here # they are `,`	*Paste here* # I will `,`
Paste here # we are `,`	*Paste here* # he will `,`
Paste here # I have `,`	*Paste here* # she will `,`
Paste here # they have `,`	*Paste here* # we will `,`
Paste here # we have `,`	*Paste here* # they will `,`

From *The Sound Sleuth.* Copyright © 1998 Good Year Books.

Contractions Card Match

Name _____   **Date** _____

Cut out the cards and match them to the contractions on the game board.

Contraction Cards

they'll	who's	I'll
we'll	he's	she'll
you'll	we're	it's
they're	I'm	where's

Contraction Game Board

they are	it is	we will
he is	I am	I will
you will	we are	they will
she will	where is	who is

From *The Sound Sleuth*. Copyright © 1998 Good Year Books.

Syllable Drums

Name _____ **Date** _____

Clap out these words. How many beats do they have?

baby

drum

play

playing

dog

syllable

Draw dots on the drums to show how many beats there are in each word.

dictionary

letter

From *The Sound Sleuth*. Copyright © 1998 Good Year Books.

Syllable Claps

Name _____   **Date** _____

Clap out five of your friends' names. Write a name and the number of beats in it in each hand.

That's me.

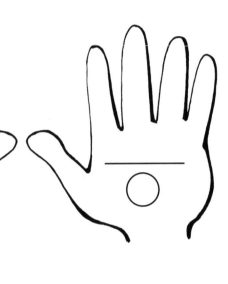

Watson
②

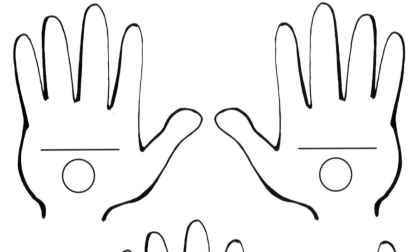

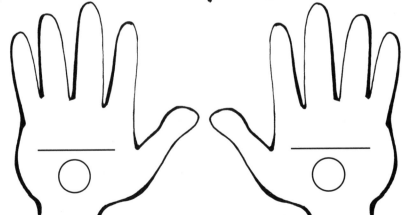

From *The Sound Sleuth*. Copyright © 1998 Good Year Books.

Opposite Match

Name _____ **Date** _____

Cut out these cards and match them to the cards on the next page.

From *The Sound Sleuth*. Copyright © 1998 Good Year Books.

little	fast
full	float
night	thin
close	short
under	hot

Opposite Match

Name _____   **Date** _____

Cut out these cards to match to the opposites on page 67.

big

slow

empty

sink

day

thick

open

tall

over

cold

From *The Sound Sleuth.* Copyright © 1998 Good Year Books.

Synonym Book

Name _____ **Date** _____

Make a book of synonyms.

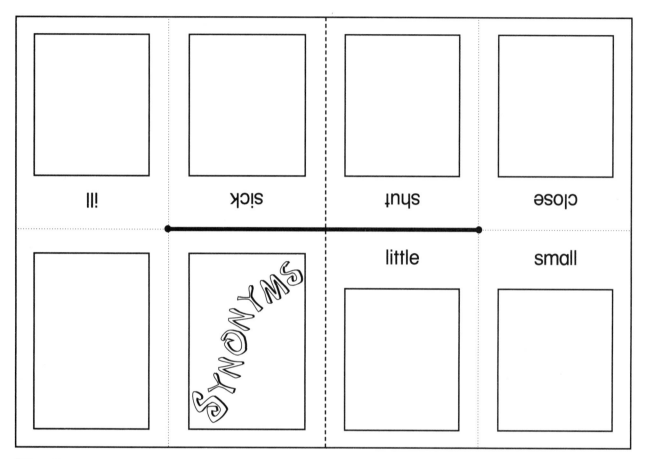

Directions

1. Fold along all lines. Open the paper again.

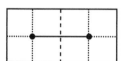

2. Fold along the line with the dashes. Cut along the thick black line.

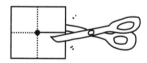

3. Open the sheet and fold along the line with the cut.

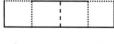

4. Push the left and right edges together to make the large black dots meet.

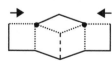

5. Flatten the pages and fold into a book with the cover on the front. Draw pictures for the words.

From *The Sound Sleuth*. Copyright © 1998 Good Year Books.

Homonym Poster

Name _____   **Date** _____

```
┌─────────────────────────────────────────────────────────────┐
│                    ┌──────────────────────┐                  │
│                    │                      │                  │
│                    └──────────────────────┘                  │
│                              │                               │
│                              │                               │
│                              │                               │
│                              │                               │
│                              │                               │
│                              │                               │
│                              │                               │
└─────────────────────────────────────────────────────────────┘
```

Pick two words that sound the same and make a poster.

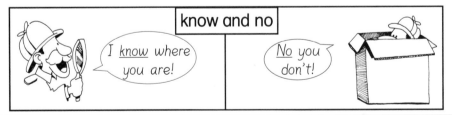

know and no

I *know* where you are!

No you don't!

meet and meat	blue and blew
here and hear	son and sun
right and write	steel and steal

From *The Sound Sleuth.* Copyright © 1998 Good Year Books.

Two or To

Name _____ **Date** _____

Circle **to** or **two** in these sentences.

I went (to / two) the park.

I have (to / two) apples.

My brother is (to / two) years old.

He goes (to / two) school.

She likes (to / two) read.

One and one is (to / two).

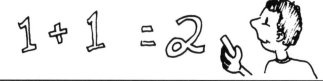

From *The Sound Sleuth*. Copyright © 1998 Good Year Books.

Too (As Well)

Name _____ **Date** _____

May I come too?

Paste *too* over *as well*. Read the new sentences.

1. too	He's having some cake and I'm having some as well.
2. too	She's going to the zoo and we're going as well.
3. too	He has three books and I have three as well.
4. too	If you go to the store may I go as well?
5. too	When they do their work, I work as well.

From *The Sound Sleuth*. Copyright © 1998 Good Year Books.

To or Too (More than Enough)

Name _____   **Date** _____

Watson hid **to** and **too** from these sentences in the backyard. Help Watson
remember where he buried the missing words.

I will go_____the shop.

The ice cream is_____cold.

The bed is_____hard.

I went_____the beach.

This shirt is_____big for me.

I sent a letter_____my friend.

I'll find
them.

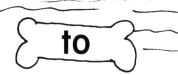 to   too   too

to   too   to

From *The Sound Sleuth*. Copyright © 1998 Good Year Books.

Adjectives

Name _____ **Date** _____

Slide the adjective strip through the slots in the sentence to
find out what Watson is like. Write an adjective of your own.

Watson is a _____ dog.

fold along
dotted line

cut

cut

playful

happy

friendly

fast

clever

_____

From *The Sound Sleuth.* Copyright © 1998 Good Year Books.

True or False?

Name _____ **Date** _____

Read the sentences and circle true or false.

Hey! How're you doing? Want to go for a walk? Let's go!

| Dogs can talk. | true |
| | false |

| Cats drink milk. | true |
| | false |

| Tigers sleep in beds. | true |
| | false |

| Elephants can fly. | true |
| | false |

| Mice like cheese. | true |
| | false |

From *The Sound Sleuth*. Copyright © 1998 Good Year Books.

Name _____   **Date** _____

Watson is a good pet

He is clever   He plays

games   He can catch

a ball   He likes to listen

to stories

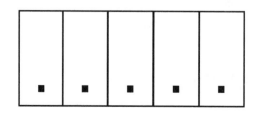

From *The Sound Sleuth*. Copyright © 1998 Good Year Books.

Question Marks

Name _____   **Date** _____

Paste or draw the question marks at the end of the riddles. Then solve the riddles.

I am small. I have 8 legs.
What am I ☐ A _____.

I live in a pond. I eat bugs.
What am I ☐ A _____.

I am furry. I say meow.
What am I ☐ A _____.

I have 4 legs. I have a very long
neck. What am I ☐ A _____.

❓❓❓❓

From *The Sound Sleuth*. Copyright © 1998 Good Year Books.

Questions and Answers

Name _____   **Date** _____

Read the questions, and then underline each correct answer.

Can dogs run?	yes no	
Can a cow sing?	yes no	
Can you eat a house?	yes no	
Do cats have whiskers?	yes no	
Does a fish have fur?	yes no	
Can birds fly?	yes no	
Do pigs bark?	yes no	

From *The Sound Sleuth*. Copyright © 1998 Good Year Books.

Quotation Marks

Name _____ **Date** _____

Paste or draw " at the beginning and " at the end of what Watson and Spot say.

☐ Hello, ☐ said Watson.

Hello

☐ Hello, ☐ said Spot.

Hello

☐ I'm looking for bones, ☐ said Watson.

I'm looking for bones

☐ May I look too? ☐ asked Spot.

May I look too?

☐ Yes, ☐ said Watson.

Yes

" " " " " " " " " "

From *The Sound Sleuth*. Copyright © 1998 Good Year Books.

Quotation Marks

Name _____   **Date** _____

Cut out and tape these signs onto rulers to use in stories or plays.

From *The Sound Sleuth*. Copyright © 1998 Good Year Books.

Exclamation Marks

Name _____   **Date** _____

Trace the exclamation marks and then read what the dogs are saying.

"Help!" yelled Watson.

From *The Sound Sleuth.* Copyright © 1998 Good Year Books.

Help!

"Where are you Watson?" asked Spot.

Where are you?

"I'm over here!" yelled Watson.

I'm over here!

"I'm caught in this bush!" shouted Spot.

I'm caught in this bush!

Apostrophe to Show Possession

Name _____   **Date** _____

The bone belongs to Watson.
It is Watson's bone.

*The apostrophe before the **s** shows the bone belongs to me.*

Cut out the labels and paste them next to things belonging to Watson in the picture below.

Watson's feet	Watson's bowl	Watson's ears
Watson's nose	Watson's tail	Watson's doghouse

From *The Sound Sleuth*. Copyright © 1998 Good Year Books.

Story Sequence

Name _____   **Date** _____

Write a sentence about each picture. Put the pages in order and staple them together.

_____

_____

_____

_____

_____

_____

_____

_____

_____

_____

_____

_____

_____

_____

_____

_____

_____

_____

_____

_____

From *The Sound Sleuth*. Copyright © 1998 Good Year Books.

"Sherlock Sound Sleuth" Mask

Name _____   **Date** _____

Color and cut out the mask. Staple string or elastic thread to each *X*.

From *The Sound Sleuth*. Copyright © 1998 Good Year Books.

"Watson Word Whiz" Mask

Name _____ **Date** _____

Color and cut out the mask. Staple string or elastic thread to each *X*.

From *The Sound Sleuth*. Copyright © 1998 Good Year Books.

Magnifying Glass for Sound Hunts

Name _____   **Date** _____

Cut
out
center

Cut out the magnifying
glass and look through
it when you go on
word hunts.

From *The Sound Sleuth*. Copyright © 1998 Good Year Books.

"Sherlock Sound Sleuth" Badge and "Watson Word Whiz" Collar

Name _____   **Date** _____

Color and cut out the "Sherlock Sound Sleuth" badge and the "Watson Word Whiz" collar.

From *The Sound Sleuth*. Copyright © 1998 Good Year Books.

Achievement Certificates

Name _____   **Date** _____

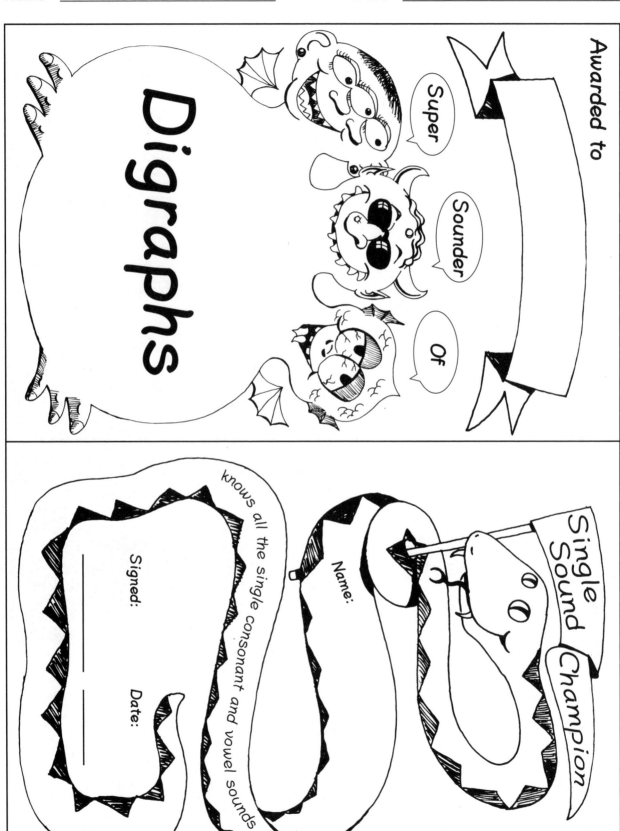

From *The Sound Sleuth*. Copyright © 1998 Good Year Books.

Achievement Certificates

Name _____   **Date** _____

From *The Sound Sleuth*. Copyright © 1998 Good Year Books.

CONGRATULATIONS

is encouraging
and cooperative
in group games.

Signed,

_____

Date _____

PRESENTED to

a true blue

WORD FAMILY WIZ